1st Level Maths

1C

Practice Workbook 2

Author: Felicity Martin
Series Consultant: Carol Lyon
Series Editor: Craig Lowther

© 2024 Leckie

001/10102024

10 9 8 7 6 5 4 3 2 1

ISBN 9780008680329

Published by
Leckie
An imprint of HarperCollins Publishers
Westerhill Road, Bishopbriggs, Glasgow, G64 2QT

T: 0844 576 8126 F: 0844 576 8131
leckiescotland@harpercollins.co.uk www.leckiescotland.co.uk

HarperCollins Publishers
Macken House, 39/40 Mayor Street Upper, Dublin 1, D01 C9W8, Ireland

Publisher: Fiona McGlade

Special thanks
Project editor: Peter Dennis
Layout: Siliconchips
Proofreader: Julianna Dunn

A CIP Catalogue record for this book is available from the British Library.

Acknowledgements
Images © Shutterstock.com

Whilst every effort has been made to trace the copyright holders, in cases where this has been unsuccessful, or if any have inadvertently been overlooked, the Publishers would gladly receive any information enabling them to rectify any error or omission at the first opportunity.

Printed in the UK by Martins the Printers

MIX
Paper | Supporting responsible forestry
FSC™ C007454
www.fsc.org

This book contains FSC™ certified paper and other controlled sources to ensure responsible forest management.

For more information visit: www.harpercollins.co.uk/green

Contents

Answers

Check your answers to this workbook online: https://collins.co.uk/pages/scottish-primary-maths

1 Find the following:

a) Three fifths of 15 eggs = ☐ eggs.

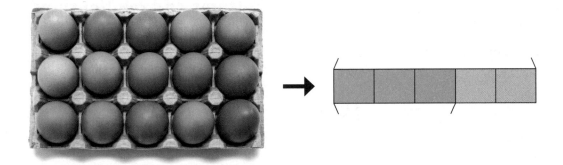

b) Five sixths of eighteen pencils = ☐ pencils.

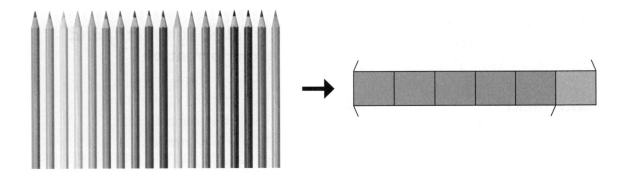

c) Five eighths of 16 bottles = ☐ bottles.

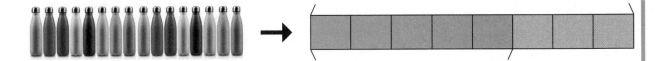

d) Three quarters of 20 cupcakes = ☐ cupcakes.

2 Draw bar models to solve:

a) Four fifths of £25.

b) Four fifths of 30 children.

c) Five ninths of 18 plants.

d) Seven ninths of 18 pebbles.

e) Four ninths of 36 bees.

f) Eight ninths of 36 socks.

3 Draw bar models to solve:

a) Amman has 32 stickers. He keeps three-quarters of them and gives the rest away. How many stickers does he have now?

☐

b) Nuria has 21 grapes in her lunchbox. She eats two-thirds of them. How many are left?

☐

c) It takes 25 minutes for Finlay to walk home from school. How many minutes does it take him to walk two-fifths of the way?

☐

★ Challenge

a) Which is bigger, three fifths of 100 or three-quarters of 80? Explain your thinking.

b) Isla thinks of a number. Four sevenths of her number is 28. What is Isla's number? Explain your thinking.

5.2 Making a whole

1 How many more of each fraction is needed to make **one whole**? Draw the fractions.

a) Two thirds

| one third $\frac{1}{3}$ | one third $\frac{1}{3}$ |

b) Two fifths

| one fifth $\frac{1}{5}$ | one fifth $\frac{1}{5}$ |

c) Four sixths

| one sixth $\frac{1}{6}$ | one sixth $\frac{1}{6}$ |
| one sixth $\frac{1}{6}$ | one sixth $\frac{1}{6}$ |

d) Four tenths

| one tenth $\frac{1}{10}$ | one tenth $\frac{1}{10}$ |
| one tenth $\frac{1}{10}$ | one tenth $\frac{1}{10}$ |

2 Fill in the blanks using these fractions from this box.

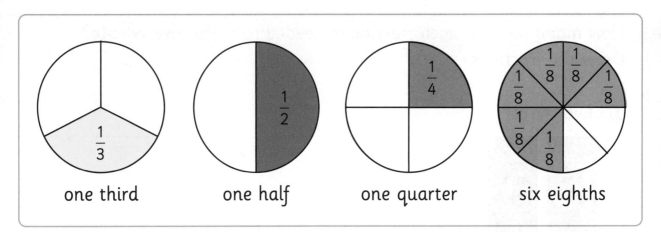

one third   one half   one quarter   six eighths

a)

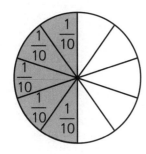

five tenths + [ ] = 1 whole

b)

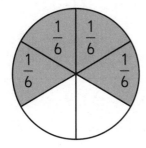

four sixths + [ ] = 1 whole

c)

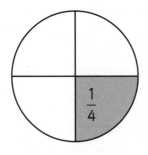

one quarter + [ ] = 1 whole

d)

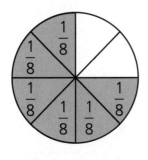

six eighths + [ ] = 1 whole

Draw lines to match the pairs of fractions that make one whole.

one fifth	one fifth	one fifth
$\frac{1}{5}$	$\frac{1}{5}$	$\frac{1}{5}$

one sixth	one sixth
$\frac{1}{6}$	$\frac{1}{6}$

one sixth	one sixth
$\frac{1}{6}$	$\frac{1}{6}$

one half
$\frac{1}{2}$

one third
$\frac{1}{3}$

one eighth	one eighth	one eighth
$\frac{1}{8}$	$\frac{1}{8}$	$\frac{1}{8}$

one eighth	one eighth	one eighth
$\frac{1}{8}$	$\frac{1}{8}$	$\frac{1}{8}$

one fifth	one fifth
$\frac{1}{5}$	$\frac{1}{5}$

one twelfth	one twelfth
$\frac{1}{12}$	$\frac{1}{12}$

one twelfth	one twelfth
$\frac{1}{12}$	$\frac{1}{12}$

one fifth	one fifth
$\frac{1}{5}$	$\frac{1}{5}$

one tenth	one tenth	one tenth
$\frac{1}{10}$	$\frac{1}{10}$	$\frac{1}{10}$

one tenth	one tenth
$\frac{1}{10}$	$\frac{1}{10}$

one tenth	one tenth	one tenth
$\frac{1}{10}$	$\frac{1}{10}$	$\frac{1}{10}$

one tenth	one tenth	one tenth
$\frac{1}{10}$	$\frac{1}{10}$	$\frac{1}{10}$

one quarter
$\frac{1}{4}$

one sixth	one sixth
$\frac{1}{6}$	$\frac{1}{6}$

one sixth	one sixth
$\frac{1}{6}$	$\frac{1}{6}$

5.3 Ordering fractions

1 Write the symbol for **greater than** > or **less than** < in the circles to make each statement true.

a) $\dfrac{1}{3}$ ◯ $\dfrac{1}{4}$

b) one ninth ◯ one tenth

c) $\dfrac{1}{50}$ ◯ $\dfrac{1}{25}$

d) one eighteenth ◯ one sixth

e) $\dfrac{1}{12}$ ◯ $\dfrac{1}{100}$

f) one sixth ◯ one fifth

2 Write the fractions shown by the arrows on each number line in the correct order.

a) $\dfrac{1}{2}, \dfrac{1}{4}, \dfrac{1}{8}, \dfrac{1}{3}$

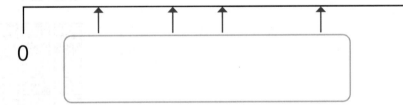

0   1

b) $\dfrac{1}{7}, \dfrac{1}{10}, \dfrac{1}{20}, \dfrac{1}{5}$

0   1

c) $\dfrac{1}{6}, \dfrac{1}{10}, \dfrac{1}{16}, \dfrac{1}{8}$

0   1

3 a) Write down four fractions that are smaller than one third.

☐ ☐ ☐ ☐

b) Now write them in order from largest to smallest. Ask a friend to check.

☐ ☐ ☐ ☐

4 a) Write down four fractions that are larger than one tenth.

☐ ☐ ☐ ☐

b) Now write them in order from largest to smallest. Ask a friend to check.

☐ ☐ ☐ ☐

★ **Challenge**

Nine sixteenths is bigger than five eighths because nine is bigger than five and sixteen is bigger than eight.

Is Nuria correct? Explain your answer.

5.4 Adding and subtracting fractions

1 How much do the girls have altogether? Draw your answer and label it. One has been done for you.

a)

9 eighths of a cake + 7 eighths of a cake = 16 eighths of a cake

= two whole cakes

b)

5 thirds of a doughnut + 4 thirds of a doughnut = ☐ thirds of a doughnut

= ☐ whole doughnuts

c)

14 sixths of a chocolate bar + 10 sixths of a chocolate bar = ☐ sixths of a chocolate bar

= ☐ whole chocolate bars

d)

17 tenths + 13 tenths = ☐ tenths

= ☐ wholes

2

a)

six sixths

I am going to eat two sixths of the pizza.

How much is left? Show your working.

b)

twelve twelfths

I am going to eat seven twelfths of the chocolate bar.

How much is left? Show your working.

3

How many wholes? Complete the fraction sentences.

a) ten eighths + six eighths = [ ] wholes.

b) twelve ninths − three ninths = [ ] wholes.

c) seven quarters + nine quarters = [ ] wholes.

d) 19 tenths − nine tenths = [ ] whole.

4 Solve these problems. Show your working.

a) There are two pizzas. Each pizza is cut into quarters. How many people can each have a quarter of a pizza?

b) Finlay gives Isla three eighths of his birthday cake. He gives Nuria five eighths of his cake. How much of the cake does Finlay get?

★ **Challenge**

Amman has five eighths of a pizza, Finlay has three quarters of a pizza and Isla has half a pizza. Isla thinks they have two whole pizzas between them. Is she right? Explain your thinking.

5.5 Creating equivalent fractions

1 Split each quarter.

a) Split each quarter into two equal parts.

| one quarter | one quarter | one quarter | one quarter |

How many equal parts altogether? [ ]

Each part is one [ ]

Four quarters is equal to [ ]

One quarter is equal to [ ]

b) Split each quarter into three equal parts.

| one quarter | one quarter | one quarter | one quarter |

How many equal parts altogether? [ ]

Each part is one [ ]

Four quarters is equal to [ ]

One quarter is equal to [ ]

c) Split each quarter into four equal parts

| one quarter | one quarter | one quarter | one quarter |

How many equal parts altogether? [ ]

Each part is one [ ]

Four quarters is equal to [ ]

One quarter is equal to [ ]

d) Split each quarter into five equal parts

| one quarter | one quarter | one quarter | one quarter |

How many equal parts altogether? [ ]

Each part is one [ ]

Four quarters is equal to [ ]

One quarter is equal to [ ]

2 Split each fifth.

a) Split each fifth into two equal parts.

one fifth	one fifth	one fifth	one fifth	one fifth

How many equal parts altogether?

Each part is one

Five fifths is equal to

One fifth is equal to

b) Split each fifth into three equal parts.

one fifth	one fifth	one fifth	one fifth	one fifth

How many equal parts altogether?

Each part is one

Five fifths is equal to

One fifth is equal to

c) Split each fifth into four equal parts.

one fifth	one fifth	one fifth	one fifth	one fifth

How many equal parts altogether?

Each part is one

Five fifths is equal to

One fifth is equal to

3 Complete the missing numerator. You could use objects, a fraction wall or drawings to help you.

a) $\frac{1}{5} = \frac{\boxed{}}{10}$

b) $\frac{1}{4} = \frac{\boxed{}}{12}$

c) $\frac{1}{3} = \frac{\boxed{}}{12}$

d) $\frac{1}{6} = \frac{\boxed{}}{12}$

4 Complete the missing denominator. You could use objects, a fraction wall or drawings to help you.

a) $\frac{1}{2} = \frac{5}{\boxed{}}$

b) $\frac{1}{4} = \frac{4}{\boxed{}}$

c) $\frac{1}{5} = \frac{4}{\boxed{}}$

d) $\frac{1}{3} = \frac{2}{\boxed{}}$

★ **Challenge**

Which is the odd one out? Explain your thinking.

| $\frac{40}{100}$ | $\frac{8}{20}$ | $\frac{4}{5}$ | $\frac{20}{50}$ | $\frac{4}{10}$ |

1 Which is larger? Tick the larger fraction.

a) Which is larger, one quarter of the first circle or one third of the second circle?

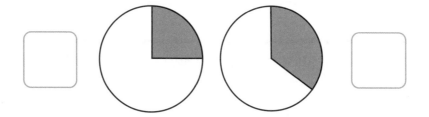

b) Which is larger, one quarter of the circle on the left or one third of the circle on the right?

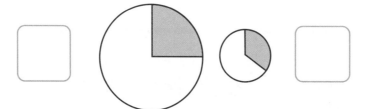

2 Write a sentence to compare the following diagrams.

a)

b)

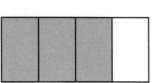 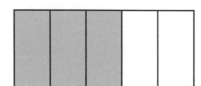

3 Draw diagrams to prove that:

a) One half can sometimes be smaller than one fifth.

b) Five eighths can sometimes be smaller than five sixths.

c) Three tenths can sometimes be larger than three quarters.

d) Four fifths can sometimes be smaller than four ninths.

★ **Challenge**

Amman has twice as much money as Nuria.
Nuria has twice as much money as Finlay.

Isla can have:

A – all of Finlay's money OR

B – half of Finlay's money and a quarter of Nuria's money OR

C – an eighth of Amman's money and an eighth of Finlay's money.

Which option will give Isla the most money? Show your thinking.

5.7 Find a fraction of an amount

1

a) $\frac{1}{3}$ of 60 = ⬚　　b) $\frac{1}{5}$ of 15 = ⬚　　c) $\frac{1}{4}$ of 16 = ⬚

2 Solve these problems using division and multiplication. One has been done for you.

a)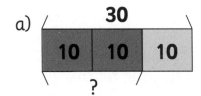

$\frac{1}{3}$ of 30 = 10

$\frac{2}{3}$ of 30 = 2 × 10 = 20

b)

18

| 6 | | |

?

$\frac{1}{3}$ of 18 = 6

$\frac{2}{3}$ of 18 = 2 × 6 = ⬚

c)

30

?

$\frac{1}{5}$ of 30 = ⬚

$\frac{2}{5}$ of 30 = 2 × ⬚ = ⬚

d)

45

?

$\frac{1}{5}$ of 45 = ⬚

$\frac{2}{5}$ of 45 = ⬚ × ⬚ = ⬚

e)

18

?

$\frac{1}{6}$ of 18 = ⬚

$\frac{2}{6}$ of 18 = ⬚

f)

42

?

$\frac{1}{6}$ of 42 = ⬚

$\frac{2}{6}$ of 42 = ⬚

3 Solve:

a) $\frac{1}{3}$ of 21 notebooks is [ ] , so $\frac{2}{3}$ of 21 notebooks is [ ]

b) $\frac{1}{5}$ of 25 rubbers is [ ] , so $\frac{3}{5}$ of 25 rubbers is [ ]

c) $\frac{1}{8}$ of 40 stickers is [ ] , so $\frac{3}{8}$ of 40 stickers is [ ]

4 Write number stories for each of the following:

a) Nuria is watching TV. Her programme lasts for 50 minutes and she has watched $\frac{3}{10}$ of it. How long has Nuria been watching? [ ]

b) Finlay is looking at fish in an aquarium. There are 25 fish in the aquarium and Finlay can see $\frac{3}{5}$ of them. How many fish can Finlay see? [ ]

c) Isla's house is 24 km from school. There is a post box $\frac{3}{4}$ of the way from Isla's house to school. How far is the post box from Isla's house? [ ]

★ **Challenge**

What are the missing digits? Show your working. You could use objects or drawings to help you.

a) $\frac{3}{4}$ of 40 = $\frac{\square}{5}$ of 75

b) $\frac{\square}{7}$ of 49 = $\frac{7}{8}$ of 32

5.8 Sharing one whole

1 Draw bar models to show how much each person will get.

a) One pizza to be shared equally between eight people.

Each person will get _____ of the pizza.

b) One chocolate bar to be shared equally between twelve people.

Each person will get _____ of the chocolate bar.

c) One carton of milk to be shared equally between five people.

Each person will get _____ of the milk.

d) One cake to be shared equally between ten people.

Each person will get _____ of the cake.

2 Amman and Nuria are sharing out food.

Draw bar models to show how much of each will be left for Amman if Nuria takes:

a) five eighths of the pie

b) two thirds of the water

c) seven twelfths of the bread

3 Finlay, Nuria and Isla are sharing a pizza.

Finlay takes seven sixteenths. Nuria takes five sixteenths. Isla gets the rest. How much pizza does Isla get? Show your working.

★ **Challenge**

The children have three whole cookies to share equally between the four of them.

How much will each child get?

Explain your thinking.

6.1 Recording amounts

1 Write these amounts using decimal notation.

a) £1 and 35p

b) £1 and 5p

c) £14 and 30p

d) £14

2 Write these amounts in £ and p.

a) £5.80

b) £5.08

c) £7.88

d) £37.07

3 Write down these amounts using decimal notation.

a)

b)

c)

d)

e)

f)

4 Draw the least number of notes and coins that total these amounts.

a) £6.90

b) £16.53

c) £12.38

d) £30.09

★ **Challenge**

Finlay has £12.09. What notes and coins might he have if he has:

five notes/coins

eight notes/coins

ten notes/coins

twelve notes/coins

Now work with a partner to see how many other ways you can make £12.09. Record your solutions on a whiteboard or in your jotter.

6.2 Adding amounts

1 Amman has £1.53. His mum gives him £3.20. How much does he have now? Draw this total with the fewest number of coins.

2 Total the following amounts of money:

a) 85p + £2.29

b) £1.85 + £2.27

c) £4.40 + 99p

d) £4.40 + £3.99

e) £1.27 + £3.99

f) 27p + £2.60 + £1.99

3 Nuria's dad uses his online bank account to buy three computer games. One costs £3.99 and the other two each cost £1.89. How much money does he need to have in his bank account to make sure he can pay?

4 Isla's parents are in the corner shop. They buy a newspaper, a can of soup, milk and a packet of biscuits.

£1.30   Newspaper   £1.19   £2.50   89p

They have £7 in the bank and pay for their shopping using a debit card. How much money do they have left in the bank?

★ **Challenge**

Finlay has been given a gift card for the cinema. It had £20 on it, but he has already spent some of that on a ticket to see a film last week.

Finlay wants to see a different film so he needs another ticket. A cinema ticket costs £4.99.

£3.58   £4.89   £1.55   £3.27   £2.50

What food should Finlay buy to make sure he uses the exact amount of money left on his gift card? Show your working.

6.3 Calculating change

1 Calculate the change from the notes given for when you spend the following amounts. Use the empty number lines to help you.

a) Spend £8.25

£10 £ _____ | change |

b) Spend £4.50

£20 £ _____ | change |

c) Spend £3.83

£10 £ _____ | change |

d) Spend £ 1.83

£5 £ _____ | change |

e) Spend 74p

£10 £ _____ | change |

2 Amman and Isla buy books. Draw the coins they each get as change using the least number of coins.

a) Amman buys a book that costs £7.35. He pays with a £10 note.

b) Isla buys a book that costs 98p. She pays with a £5 note.

★ **Challenge**

Nuria is buying art pencils. If she buys two pencils, she gets a third one free. Each pencil costs £2.15.

She has these coins and notes in her purse.

How many art pencils can Nuria afford to buy? Show your working.

How much change will she receive?

1 Look at the calendar and answer the questions.

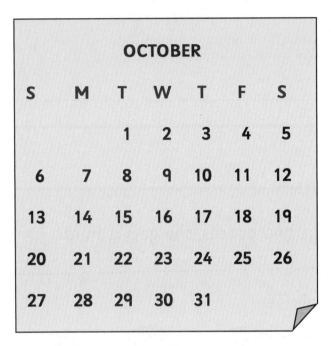

OCTOBER

S	M	T	W	T	F	S
		1	2	3	4	5
6	7	8	9	10	11	12
13	14	15	16	17	18	19
20	21	22	23	24	25	26
27	28	29	30	31		

a) What **day** is the 19th October?

b) What **date** is the first Monday in October?

c) What **day** is the 31st October?

2 Look at the calendar and answer the following questions.

JANUARY						
S	M	T	W	T	F	S
		1	2	3	4	5
6	7	8	9	10	11	12
13	14	15	16	17	18	19
20	21	22	23	24	25	26
27	28	29	30	31		

FEBRUARY						
S	M	T	W	T	F	S
					1	2
3	4	5	6	7	8	9
10	11	12	13	14	15	16
17	18	19	20	21	22	23
24	25	26	27	28		

MARCH						
S	M	T	W	T	F	S
					1	2
3	4	5	6	7	8	9
10	11	12	13	14	15	16
17	18	19	20	21	22	23
24	25	26	27	28	29	30
31						

APRIL						
S	M	T	W	T	F	S
	1	2	3	4	5	6
7	8	9	10	11	12	13
14	15	16	17	18	19	20
21	22	23	24	25	26	27
28	29	30				

MAY						
S	M	T	W	T	F	S
			1	2	3	4
5	6	7	8	9	10	11
12	13	14	15	16	17	18
19	20	21	22	23	24	25
26	27	28	29	30	31	

JUNE						
S	M	T	W	T	F	S
						1
2	3	4	5	6	7	8
9	10	11	12	13	14	15
16	17	18	19	20	21	22
23	24	25	26	27	28	29
30						

JULY						
S	M	T	W	T	F	S
	1	2	3	4	5	6
7	8	9	10	11	12	13
14	15	16	17	18	19	20
21	22	23	24	25	26	27
28	29	30	31			

AUGUST						
S	M	T	W	T	F	S
				1	2	3
4	5	6	7	8	9	10
11	12	13	14	15	16	17
18	19	20	21	22	23	24
25	26	27	28	29	30	31

SEPTEMBER						
S	M	T	W	T	F	S
1	2	3	4	5	6	7
8	9	10	11	12	13	14
15	16	17	18	19	20	21
22	23	24	25	26	27	28
29	30					

OCTOBER						
S	M	T	W	T	F	S
		1	2	3	4	5
6	7	8	9	10	11	12
13	14	15	16	17	18	19
20	21	22	23	24	25	26
27	28	29	30	31		

NOVEMBER						
S	M	T	W	T	F	S
					1	2
3	4	5	6	7	8	9
10	11	12	13	14	15	16
17	18	19	20	21	22	23
24	25	26	27	28	29	30

DECEMBER						
S	M	T	W	T	F	S
1	2	3	4	5	6	7
8	9	10	11	12	13	14
15	16	17	18	19	20	21
22	23	24	25	26	27	28
29	30	31				

a) What day is the 21st of May?

b) What is the date of the second Sunday in April?

c) What is the date of the third Friday in February? Write your answer in words and numbers.

3 Look at this calendar for the year 2050 and answer these questions:

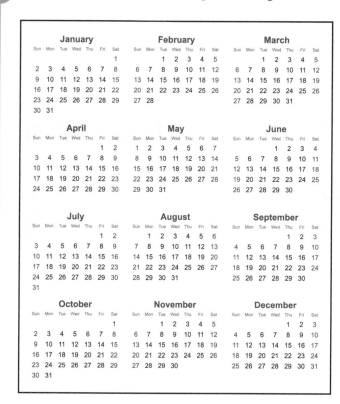

a) On what day will your birthday be in 2050?

b) How old will you be?

c) How many Thursdays are there in January 2050?

⭐ **Challenge**

Look at the calendar in question 2.

a) How many weeks are there between the 2nd June and the 16th June?

b) Amman is going on holiday. He leaves on the 4th September and returns home the following Tuesday. What date does he return? How long was his holiday, including the travel days?

c) The Edinburgh Fringe Festival lasts for exactly three weeks. If it starts on 3rd August, when does it finish?

7.2 Recording time

1 Amman's dad has entered a marathon (just over 42 km distance). Select the appropriate instrument for each part of his adventure preparation.

clock

stopwatch

calendar

a) Planning the two-night trip from Glasgow to London.

b) Timing short training sprints.

c) Planning how to get from his hotel to the start line.

d) Timing the marathon.

2 Nuria has to time how long it takes her to swim two lengths. She is not sure which instrument to use. Isla says a sand timer would be best. Finlay thinks a clock would be ideal. Amman suggests a stopwatch.

a) For each child's suggestion, say whether you agree with them or not, and **why**.

Isla:

Finlay:

Amman:

b) Amman's stopwatch reads 00:04:34. How long did Nuria take to swim a length?
Write your answer in words.

3 With a partner, decide on a distance to time. For example, from one side of the playground to the other.

Record the time it takes to do the following for this distance:

a) Run

b) Walk

c) Hop

d) Skip

Find your pulse. Use a stopwatch to count how many times your pulse beats in 15 seconds.

Now multiply this by 4 to find your heart rate in beats per minutes. Record this here.

Use the stopwatch to time yourself doing something energetic like running on the spot or doing jumping jacks for two minutes.

Now measure your pulse again.
Multiply by four and record the result here.

How much did your heart rate increase after the exercise?

_____ beats per minute.

7.3 Convert digital to analogue

1 Draw lines to match the clocks and watches which are showing the same time.

2 Write the digital time that matches the times shown on these analogue clocks.

a)

b)

c)

d)

e)

f)

3 Draw the hands on each analogue clock to make it show these times.

a) 6:15

b) 10:15

c) 10:10

d) 8:40

e) 3:40

f) 3:35

★ **Challenge**

Write the times on these clocks in order, from earliest to latest.
Record your answers in digital time.

4:35

9:15

6:25

10:10

7.4 Use a.m. and p.m. correctly

1 Say whether the following school-day activities are a.m., p.m. or both.

a) Break time ▢

b) Going home from school ▢

c) Cycling to school ▢

d) Having a friend over to play ▢

e) Taking the register ▢

f) Leaving for school ▢

2 Write a.m. or p.m. next to each time. Draw hands on the clock to show the same time.

a) 03:15 ▢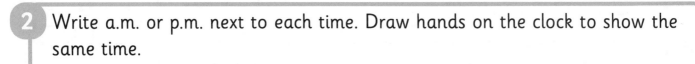

b) 12:05 ▢

c) 06:50 ▢

d) 12:45 ▢

e) 00:20 ▢

f) 10:25 ▢

3 Finlay is at a holiday camp. Fill in his plan for the day using the times and activities in the box. Remember to say a.m. or p.m.

canoeing 9:00   afternoon snack 3:30   lights out 9:00

games 8:00   breakfast 8:00   hiking 2:00

lunch 1:00   morning snack 11:00   cycling 3:45

get up 7:00   climbing 11:30   dinner 7:00

Activity	Time	a.m. / p.m.

noon is 12 a.m.

noon is 12 p.m.

So is midnight 12 am or 12 pm?

Who is right? Explain your thinking.

1 Draw lines to match each analogue clock to the correct 24-hour time.

| 1:05 | 23:55 | 17:20 | 08:45 | 15:15 | 19:20 |

2 Write the time shown on each clock in 24-hour digital notation.

a) [clock] a.m. → [   ]
p.m. → [   ]

b) [clock] a.m. → [   ]
p.m. → [   ]

c) [clock] a.m. → [   ]
p.m. → [   ]

d) [clock] a.m. → [   ]
p.m. → [   ]

e) [clock] a.m. → [   ]
p.m. → [   ]

f) [clock] a.m. → [   ]
p.m. → [   ]

3 Use the timetable to answer the questions.

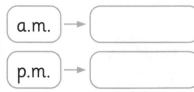

Departures		
Time	**To**	**Platform**
10:25	GLASGOW	4
11:05	ABERDEEN	7
11:45	PERTH	1
12:00	STIRLING	11
12:50	ST ANDREWS	5
13:10	INVERNESS	8
13:35	DUMFRIES	2

a) Trains to which destinations leave in the morning?

[   ]

b) Trains to which destinations leave in the afternoon?

[   ]

c) The train to St Andrews takes one hour and forty minutes.
What time will it arrive? Write your answer in 24-hour notation.

d) The train to Glasgow takes 45 minutes. What time will it arrive?
Write your answer in 24-hour notation.

★ **Challenge**

Nuria and Amman are going on holiday.
Their flight leaves at 13:35. Nuria says this
is 3:35 p.m. Amman says it is 1:35 p.m.
Who is correct? Explain your answer.

The children must be at the airport two hours before the flight leaves. It takes
an hour and a half to get to the airport from the town where they live.

a) What time must they arrive at the airport? Write your answer in 24-hour
notation. Show your working.

b) What time must they leave the house? Write your answer in 24-hour
notation. Show your working.

1 Use a ruler to measure each of these bars in centimetres.

a)

b)

c)

d)

e)

2 What is the length of each of these bars? Measure to check your answer.

a)

b)
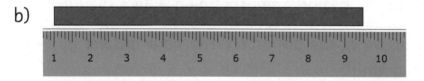

c)

d)

e)
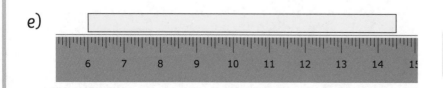

3 Draw lines that are exactly:

a) Three and a half centimetres long

b) Eight and a half centimetres long

c) One and half centimetres long

d) Four and a half centimetres long

4 With a partner, choose a wall to measure from. Measure and mark the distance that is exactly:

a) Two and a half metres from the wall.

b) Five and a half metres from the wall.

★ Challenge

Finlay is measuring the width of the gym hall. Unfortunately, he only has a broken metre stick. His stick is now sixty-five centimetres long.

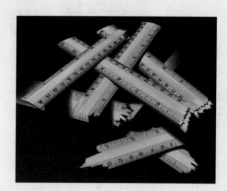

The gym hall measures thirty of Finlay's measuring sticks plus another two metres and 50 cm.

How wide is the gym hall? Show your working.

1 Measure these bars. What is the **length** of each bar in millimetres?

a)

b)

c)

d)

2 Measure the **length** of these toys, to the nearest millimetre.

a)

b)

3 Measure the **height** of these toys, to the nearest millimetre.

a)

b)

4 Draw lines that measure exactly:

a) 65 millimetres

b) 14 millimetres

c) 98 millimetres

d) 27 millimetres

e) 102 millimetres

★ Challenge

Here is a scale model of the Eiffel Tower.
The real Eiffel Tower is in France and it is very tall!

To find out the height of the real Eiffel Tower,
first multiply the height of the model (in centimetres) by 3.
Now multiply this number by 10. This is the height in metres.

How high is the real Eiffel Tower? Show your working

Work with a partner. What else can you find out about the Eiffel Tower?

1 A palaeontologist is measuring dinosaur teeth. Help him by converting the measurements into millimetres.

a)

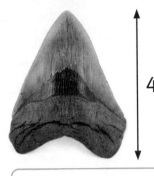

4 cm

[ ]

b)

$7\frac{1}{2}$ cm

[ ]

c)

$5\frac{1}{2}$ cm

[ ]

d)

2 cm

[ ]

2 Convert the following measurements into centimetres and millimetres. One has been done for you.

a) 74 mm = | 7 cm and 4 mm |

b) 35 mm = [ ]

c) 68 mm = [ ]

d) 114 mm = [ ]

e) 172 mm = [ ]

f) 11 mm = [ ]

3 Measure the length of each piece of string. Record your answers in two ways. One has been done for you.

a) _____

| 35 mm | 3 cm and 5 mm |

b) _____

| | |

c) _____

| | |

d) _____

| | |

e) ____

| | |

f) _____

| | |

Find these objects, or similar, in your classroom or home:

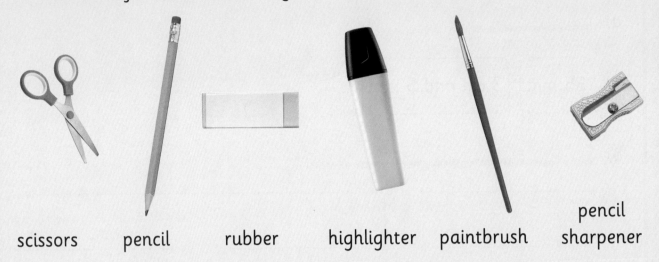

scissors   pencil   rubber   highlighter   paintbrush   pencil
                                                                                  sharpener

Estimate how long each object is in millimetres. Write down your estimate in the table.

Now measure the actual length of each object in millimetres.
Write the answer in millimetres **and** in centimetres and millimetres.

Object	Estimate	Actual length in mm	Actual length in cm and mm

8.4 Reading and recording measurements for mass

1 What is the mass of the following items in kilograms?

a)

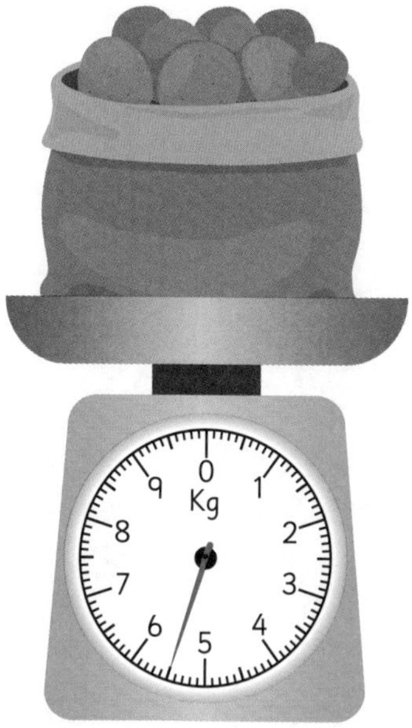

b)

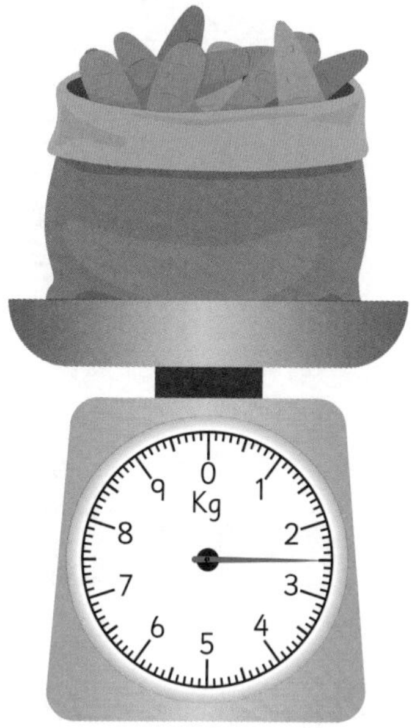

c)

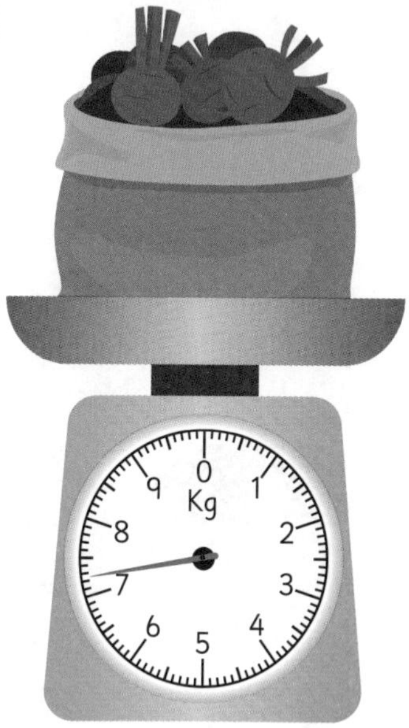

d)

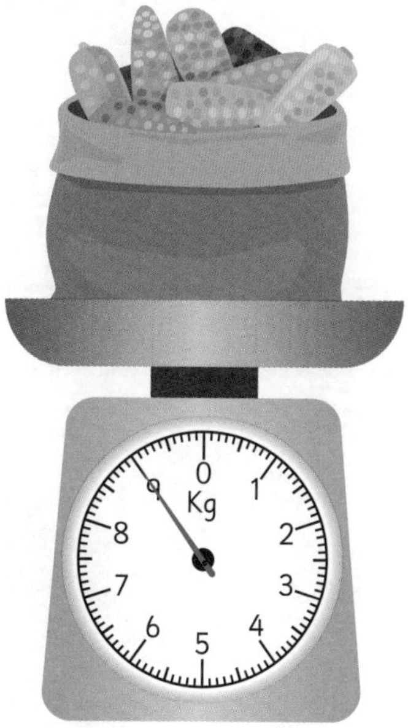

e)

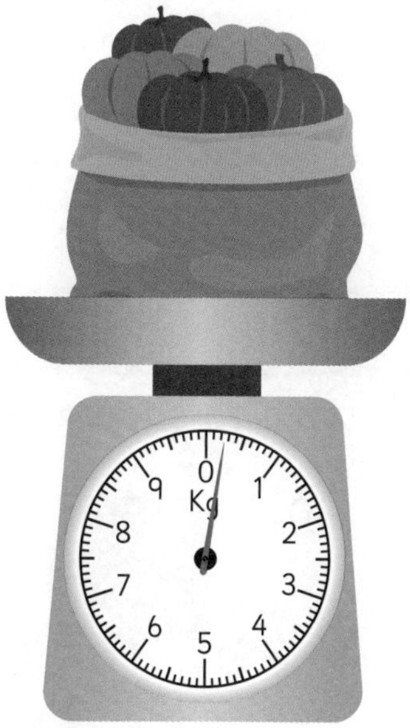

f)

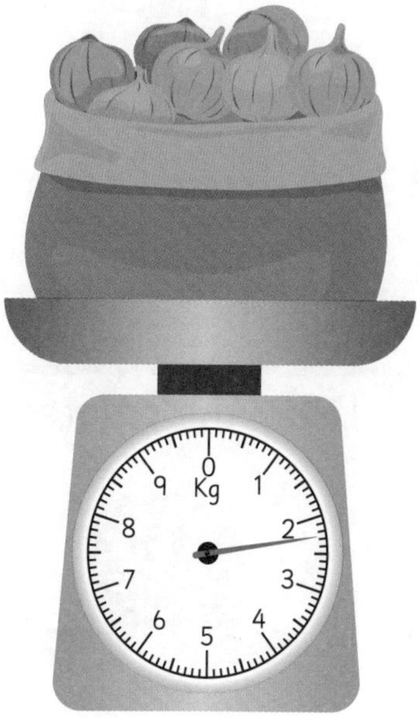

2 What is in each box? Draw lines to match the fruit to the correct scale.

a)

b)

c)

$2\frac{1}{2}$ kg of plums

750 g of pears

2kg 250 g of lemons

$1\frac{1}{4}$ kg of cherries

$\frac{1}{2}$ kg of apricots

1 kg 750 g of apples

d)

e)

f)

3 Draw the pointer on each scale to show the given mass.

a)

b)

c)

4 kg 500 g

5 kg 250 g

1 kg 500 g

d)

8 kg 750 g

e)

6 kg 250 g

★ Challenge

Ask a partner to fill boxes or bags with objects and label them A, B, C and D.

Each box or bag should weigh an exact number of kilograms and half kilograms.

They should do this without you seeing.

Compare the mass of each box or bag by picking them up.

Order the boxes and bags from lightest to heaviest.

Now estimate the actual mass of each box or bag in kilograms and record your estimates in the table.

Box/bag	A	B	C	D
Estimate				
Actual mass				

Check your estimates by weighing and complete the table.

How accurate were your estimates?

1 Write each label under the correct container.

$\frac{1}{2}$ l	$2\frac{1}{2}$ l	$1\frac{3}{4}$ l	$2\frac{1}{4}$ l	2 l	$1\frac{1}{2}$ l

a)

b)

c)

d)

e)

f)

2 Write the volume of water in each container in litres.

a)

b)

c)

d)

e)

f)

3 Draw liquid in each jug to show the correct volume.

a) $\frac{1}{4}$ litres

b) $5\frac{1}{2}$ litres

c) $4\frac{3}{4}$ litres

d) $3\frac{1}{4}$ litres

★ Challenge

Fill an unmarked container with water. Estimate the volume of water, to the nearest $\frac{1}{4}$ litre, and record in the table below.

Now pour the water into a measuring jug and write down the actual volume in the table (to the nearest $\frac{1}{4}$ litre).

Do this again for five different unmarked containers.

Container	1	2	3	4	5	6
Estimate						
Actual volume						

Compare your estimates with your actual measurements.
Do your estimates get more accurate with practice?

1 Convert:

a) The length of the lorry to centimetres.

4 m 75 cm

[   ]

b) The length of the flower to centimetres.

300 mm

[   ]

c) The length of the £10 note to millimetres.

13 cm 2 mm

[   ]

d) The length of the racing car to metres and centimetres.

560 cm

[   ]

2 State the following capacities in millilitres.

a)

3 l

[   ]

b)

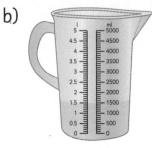

1 l and 500 ml

[   ]

c)

1 l and 750 ml

[   ]

3 State the following capacities in litres.

a)

2000 ml

[ ]

b)

4000 ml

[ ]

c)

1800 ml

[ ]

★ **Challenge**

Investigate the link between capacity and mass.

Weigh an empty measuring jug.

Pour a quantity of water into a measuring jug and record the capacity.

Next, weigh the jug with water in and subtract the weight of the empty jug. Record your findings.

Repeat for different quantities of water.

Capacity					
Mass					

What do you notice?

[   ]

Is the same thing true for things that are not water? Try, for example, flour, sugar, sand, or other liquids.

8.7 Area of shapes

1 Find the area of the following shapes in squares.

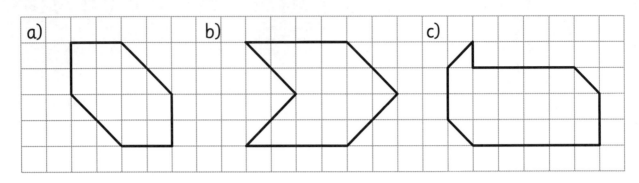

a) [ ]   b) [ ]   c) [ ]

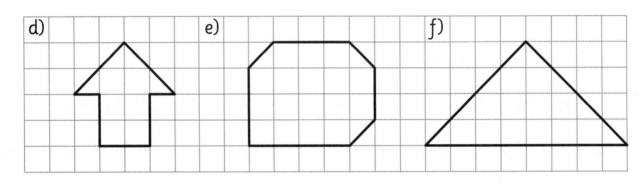

d) [ ]   e) [ ]   f) [ ]

2 i) **Estimate** how many 1 cm squares will fit onto each shape.

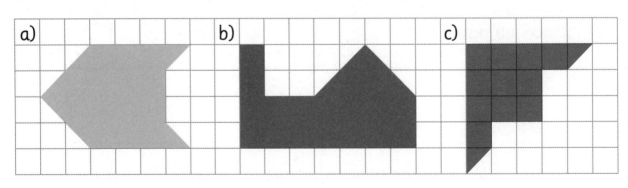

Estimate: [ ]   Estimate: [ ]   Estimate: [ ]

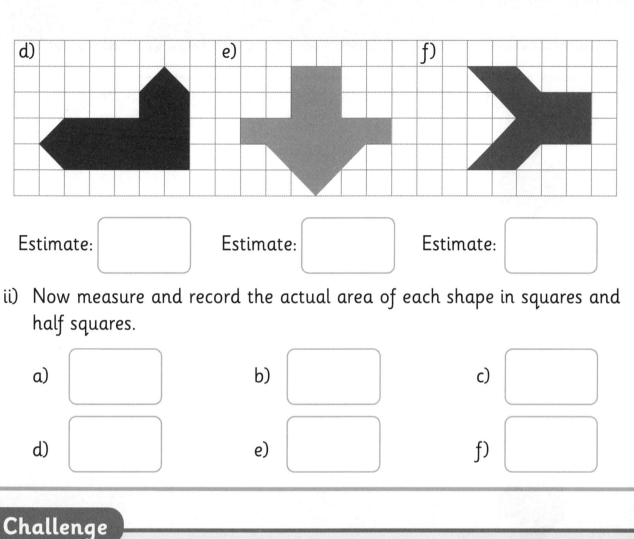

d)   e)   f)

Estimate: [   ]   Estimate: [   ]   Estimate: [   ]

ii) Now measure and record the actual area of each shape in squares and half squares.

a) [   ]   b) [   ]   c) [   ]

d) [   ]   e) [   ]   f) [   ]

★ Challenge

To find the area of a shape you can cut it up and put the parts into rectangles.

What is the area of this shape? Explain how you worked it out.

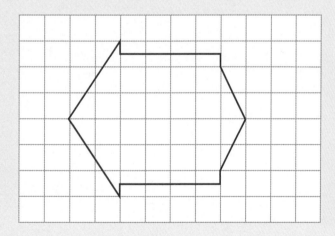

[   ]

8.8 Creating areas

1 Draw two **different** shapes with the same area as the following.

a)

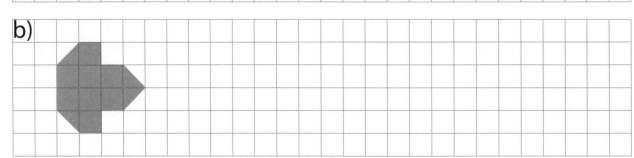

b)

c)

2 Draw at least three different shapes with the following areas. Each shape must include at least two half squares.

a) $6\frac{1}{2}$ squares

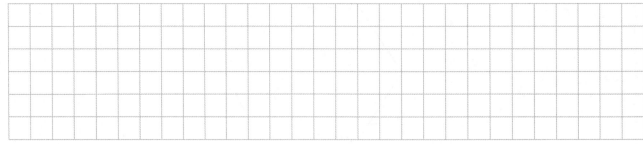

b) 14 squares

c) 11 squares

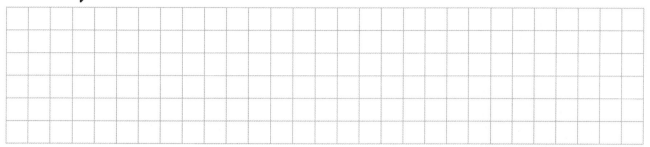

d) $18\frac{1}{2}$ squares

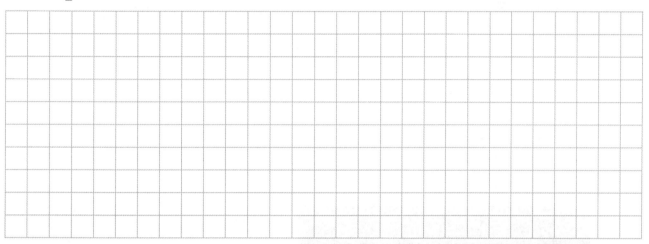

★ **Challenge**

You will need squared paper.

Pentominoes have an area of 5 squares. Whole squares only are used to make each pentomino. All the squares must touch along at least one edge.

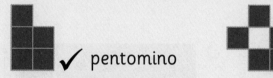 ✓ pentomino   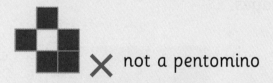 ✗ not a pentomino

Here is the same pentomino again in different orientations.

There are twelve possible pentominoes. Can you draw all twelve **different** pentominoes?

8.9 Area and arrays

1 Describe the area of each shape and write the number story. One has been done for you.

a)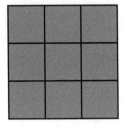

b)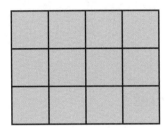

> 3 rows of 3 squares
>
> 3 × 3 = 9

c)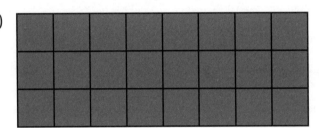

2 Write a number story to show how many green squares ▢ would fit into each of these shapes.

a)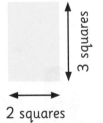

2 squares · 3 squares

b)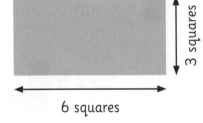

6 squares · 3 squares

c)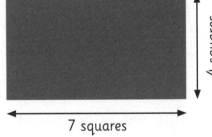

7 squares · 4 squares

This square has an area of 1. 1 × 1 = **1**

This square has an area of 4. 2 × 2 = **4**

Draw the next five squares in the sequence.
Write the number stories inside each square.

Can you predict the next three numbers in the sequence of square numbers?
Explain your thinking.

Quipus

The Incas lived around 500 AD in Peru, in South America. Quipus were a useful way of recording how many animals they had, or how much gold. The counting system involved tying knots on long pieces of string. Different coloured strings probably represented different items.

An Incan Quipu

Each number was represented by a knot. One knot = one, two knots = two and so on.

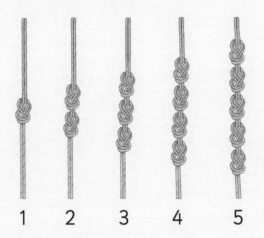

1   2   3   4   5

The place value of the numbers was shown by where they were placed on the string. The ones were at the bottom of the string, then the tens, then hundreds and so on. Instead of zero as a placeholder, they used an empty space. If there were four knots in the tens space, it meant forty.

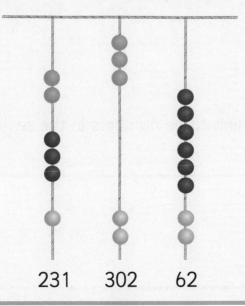

231   302   62

1 What numbers do these strings represent?

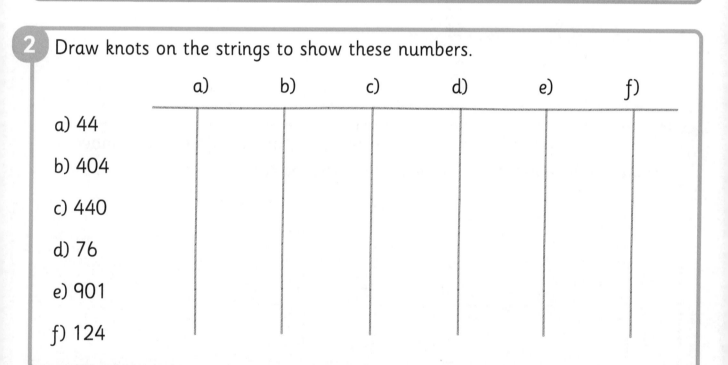

a)   b)   c)   d)   e)   f)

2 Draw knots on the strings to show these numbers.

a)   b)   c)   d)   e)   f)

a) 44

b) 404

c) 440

d) 76

e) 901

f) 124

★ **Challenge**

Make your own quipu!

Count different items in your classroom or home and record the amounts on your quipu.

Use different colours of string for different items. You could use beads instead of knots!

1 Draw the next pattern in each shape sequence.

a)

b)

c)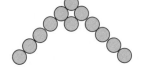

d)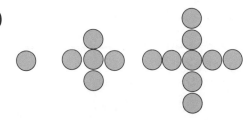

2 For each shape sequence above, write down then continue the number sequence it represents. Two have been started for you.

a) | 3 |, | 5 |, | 7 |, | 9 |, | |, | |

b) | 10 |, | |, | |, | |, | |, | |

c) | |, | |, | |, | |, | |, | |

d) | |, | |, | |, | |, | |, | |

3 Continue each of these number sequences.

a) 11, 13, 15, 17,

b) 1, 5, 9, 13,

c) 100, 92, 84, 76, ▢ ▢ ▢ ▢ ▢

d) 150, 125, 100, 75, ▢ ▢ ▢ ▢ ▢

e) 55, 46, 37, 28, ▢ ▢ ▢ ▢ ▢

4 Write the missing number in each sequence.

a) 1, 10, ▢, 28

b) 44, 39, ▢, 29

c) 19, 30, ▢, 52

d) 101, 95, ▢, 83

★ Challenge

a) Finlay creates a number sequence using the rule that the number doubles each time.

He starts with 3. What are the next **six** numbers in the sequence?

b) Amman creates a number sequence using the rule that the number halves each time.

He starts with 100. What are the next **four** numbers in the sequence?

c) Create your own number sequence and build a shape pattern to represent it. You could use cubes, straws or counters, or draw the patterns. Ask a partner to explain the rule.

10.2 Explain the rules for simple number sequences

1 Start at 6. Then use the rule given to write down the next five terms of the sequence.

a) Add 4　6 , ☐ , ☐ , ☐ , ☐ , ☐

b) Add 11　6 , ☐ , ☐ , ☐ , ☐ , ☐

c) Add 25　6 , ☐ , ☐ , ☐ , ☐ , ☐

d) Double　6 , ☐ , ☐ , ☐ , ☐ , ☐

2 Start at 120. Then use the rule given to write down the next five terms of the sequence.

a) Subtract 20　120 , ☐ , ☐ , ☐ , ☐ , ☐

b) Subtract 9　120 , ☐ , ☐ , ☐ , ☐ , ☐

c) Add 110　120 , ☐ , ☐ , ☐ , ☐ , ☐

d) Subtract 12　120 , ☐ , ☐ , ☐ , ☐ , ☐

3 Look at the first five terms of these number sequences. Write down the rule for each one.

a) 7, 15, 23, 31, 39　　Rule: ☐

b) 40, 30, 20, 10, 0　　Rule: ☐

c) 101, 92, 83, 74, 65　Rule: ☐

d) 2, 17, 32, 47, 62　　Rule: ☐

4 Work out the rules, then find the missing numbers and write them in the spaces.

a) 3 , 10 , ___ , 24 , 31   Rule: ___

b) 140 , 110 , 80 , ___ , 20   Rule: ___

c) 17 , 13 , ___ , 5 , 1   Rule: ___

d) 3 , 6 , 12 , ___ , 48   Rule: ___

e) 400 , 200 , ___ , 50 , 25   Rule: ___

★ Challenge

Here are two of the first five terms of a sequence. The sequence is made by adding the same amount each time.

4 , ___ , ___ , ___ , 20

What is the rule? What are the missing numbers? Show your working.

Create your own number sequence problem and challenge a partner to find the rule.

11.1 Completing number sentences

1 Complete these number sentences.

a) $9 + \boxed{} = 17$

b) $15 - \boxed{} = 8$

c) $\boxed{} + 18 = 25$

d) $\boxed{} - 7 = 11$

e) $15 \div \boxed{} = 3$

f) $\boxed{} = 7 \times 3$

g) $30 = 5 \times \boxed{}$

h) $\boxed{} = 6 + 9$

i) $20 \div 5 = 15 - \boxed{}$

2 If $\bullet = 3$ and $\blacktriangle = 7$, complete these equations:

a) $5 + \boxed{} = 12$

b) $5 \times \boxed{} = 15$

c) $\boxed{} - 4 = \bullet$

d) $\boxed{} \times \blacktriangle = 21$

e) $18 \div \bullet = \boxed{} - 1$

f) $12 - \boxed{} = 25 \div 5$

3 If $\bullet$ represents + and $\bullet$ represents −, complete these equations:

a) $15 \boxed{} 6 = 9$

b) $10 \boxed{} 6 = 16$

c) $15 \boxed{} 14 = 29$

d) $19 \boxed{} 3 = 16$

4 If represents × and represents ÷, complete these equations:

a) 3 ☐ 7 = 21

b) 14 ☐ 2 = 7

c) 18 ☐ 6 = 3

d) 4 ☐ 6 = 24

★ **Challenge**

◆ = 2, ⬟ = 5 and ♥ = 10

Complete each equation using the shapes, then write the equations using numbers.

a) ☐ + ☐ = ♥   ☐ + ☐ = ☐

b) ☐ × ☐ = ♥   ☐ × ☐ = ☐

c) ☐ − ☐ = ⬟   ☐ − ☐ = ☐

d) ☐ ÷ ☐ = ⬟   ☐ ÷ ☐ = ☐

Now choose your own numbers and symbols and make up your own equations for a partner to solve. Make sure you work out the answers first so you can tell them if they're right or wrong!

12.1 Sorting 3D objects

1 Circle the 3D objects where the number of faces is equal to the number of vertices.

2 Complete the Venn diagram by writing the letter of the 3D object in the correct place.

A   B   C   D

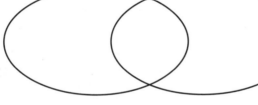

is a prism   has at least one square face

3 Complete the table by writing the letter of each object in the correct place.

A    B    C   D    E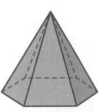

F    G   H   I   J

	Has fewer than 6 vertices	Has more than 8 edges
Is a pyramid		
Is not a pyramid		

4 Look at the 3D objects A, B, C, F, G and I in question 3. Complete the table.

	Name of object	Number of vertices	Number of edges	Number of faces
A				
B				
C				
F				
G				
I				

★ **Challenge**

Finlay and Nuria are discussing prisms and pyramids. Finlay says that an object can be both a pyramid and a prism. Nuria says that a pyramid can never be a prism.

Who is right? Explain why. You might want to draw diagrams to help you.

12.2 Plan drawings

1 Here is a drawing of a 3D object from the side.

What could it be?

Circle all the possibilities.

cone	triangle-based pyramid	cube	cylinder	triangular prism	square-based pyramid

2 Here is one part of a plan drawing of a 3D object.

List the names of regular 3D objects that look like this from the top or side or front or bottom.

3 Sketch the front, side and top view of each of these 3D objects. Use actual objects to help you. Use a ruler to draw straight lines. A right-angle tester might also be useful.

A   B   C   D

	front view	side view	top view
A			

	front view	side view	top view
B			
C			
D			

★ **Challenge**

a) The flat faces of these prisms are all the same length. Sketch the side views of each of these prisms.

Top view				
Side view				

b) What do you notice?

c) Can you predict what the side view of a decagon (10-sided) prism would look like? Sketch it in the box.

1 Continue the tiling patterns.

a)

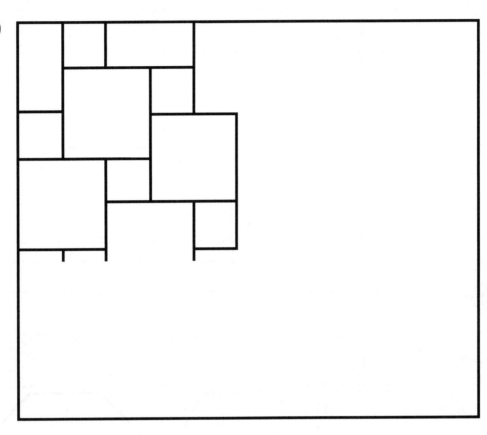

b)

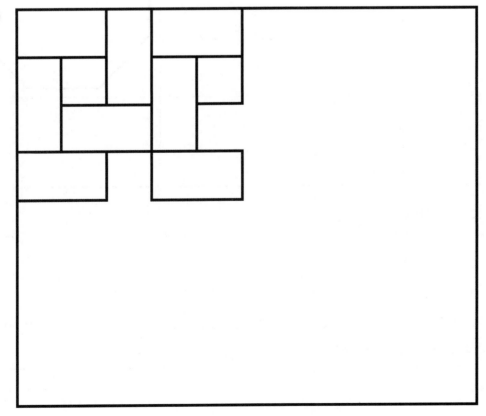

c)

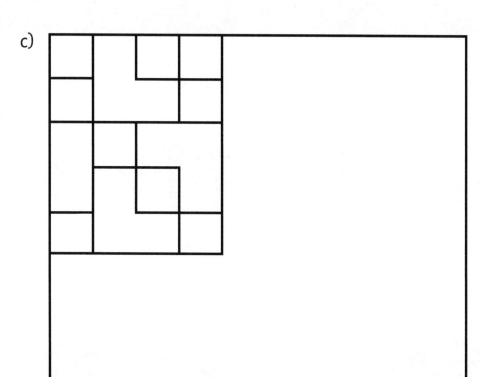

d)

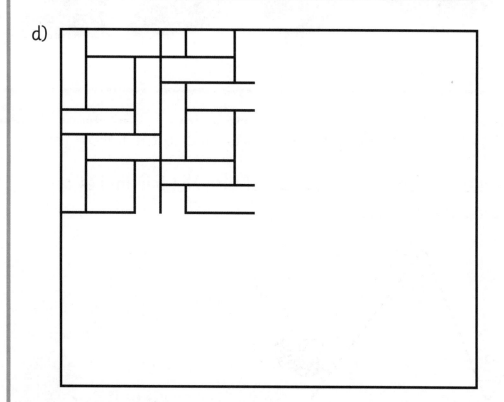

★ **Challenge**

You will need some pieces of plain or squared paper.

Make your own tiling pattern using three shapes – a small square, a large square and a rectangle. Try experimenting with different sized shapes.

13.1 Identifying angles

1 Tick the pieces of watermelon which measure less than a right angle.

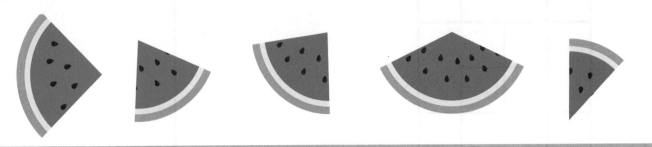

2 Tick the slices of pie which measure more than a right angle.

3 The bee starts at the red flower and flies in a zigzag line to the yellow flower.

Use a right-angle tester to check the amount of turn the bee makes at each point and complete the table.

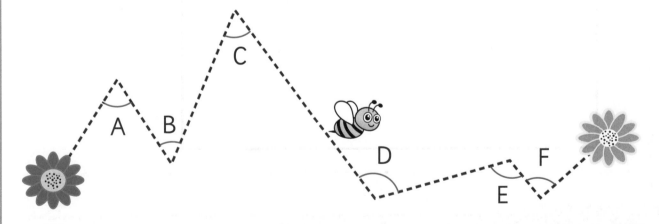

	Quarter turn	Less than a quarter turn	More than a quarter turn
Letter			

4 Draw three angles which measure less than 90° and three angles which measure more than 90°. Give them to a friend to test.

⭐ **Challenge**

A square has four straight edges that are all the same length. It has inside angles that all measure 90 degrees.

90° 90°

90° 90°

Draw a shape that has:

a) straight edges of equal length and inside angles that each measure less than 90 degrees.

b) straight edges of equal length and inside angles that each measure greater than 90 degrees.

c) straight edges of equal length, two inside angles that measure less than 90 degrees and two that measure more than 90 degrees.

1 A caterpillar goes from leaf to leaf.
Complete the directions for its route.

Forward 2
Right 90

2 A pirate is standing in B2, facing A2. He wants to reach the X, where the treasure is buried.

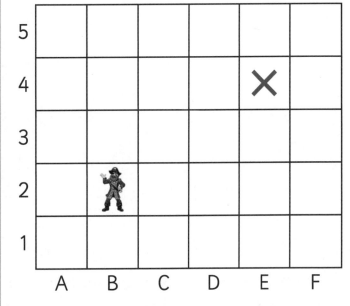

He follows these directions:

forward 1 > right 90 > forward 2 >

right 90 > forward 2 > left 90 >

forward 1 > right 90 > forward 3 >

right 90 > forward 3 > right 90 >

forward 1 > left 90 > forward 1 >

right 90 > forward 3 > right 90 >

forward 1

Does the pirate find the treasure?

If not, which square does he finish on?

Finlay has to go from square to square to get through the grid without meeting any monsters. If he enters a square next to or diagonal to a square with a monster in it, he will be eaten!

For example, he cannot go into any of these squares.

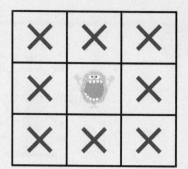

Write down the route Finlay needs to take to get him safely through the grid.

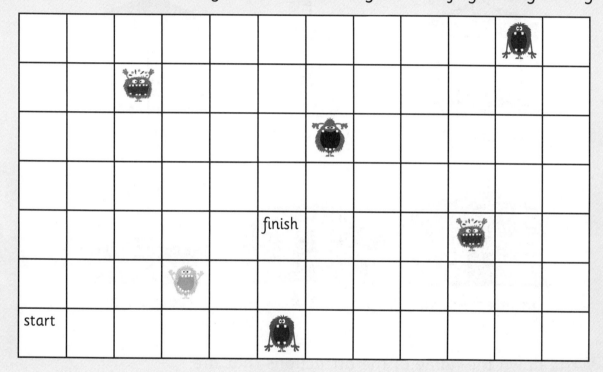

1

ferris wheel

chair swing

rollercoaster

N
W — E
S

bumper cars

ticket booth

merry-go-round

haunted house

show

teacup ride

Write down the name of the attractions that are:

a) north of the ticket booth

b) east of the show

c) west of the merry-go-round

d) south of the roller coaster

e) north of the haunted house

f) east of the ferris wheel.

2 The children are at the zoo.

		 elephants		meerkats	
reptiles			birds		
penguins		giraffes			
				bears	lemurs
	cheetahs		gorillas		

a) Isla starts at the cheetahs. She goes east
   three squares and north four squares.
   Where is she now?

b) Amman starts at the birds. He goes south
   one square then west three squares.
   Where is he now?

c) Write directions to get from the bears to the giraffes.

d) Write directions to get from the gorillas to the meerkats via the
   penguins.

3 Draw a route from the triangle to the circle. Your route must be at least ten squares long.

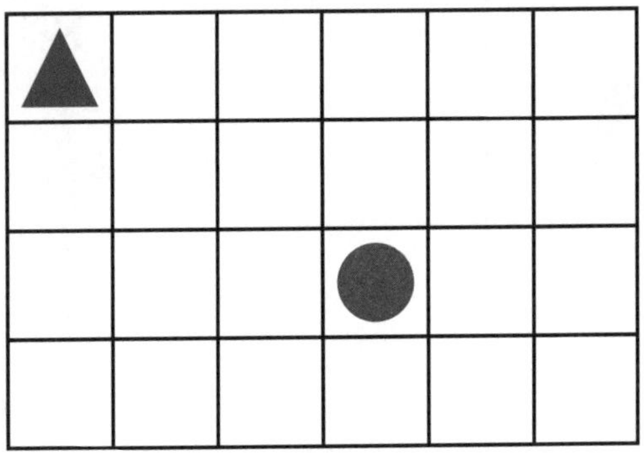

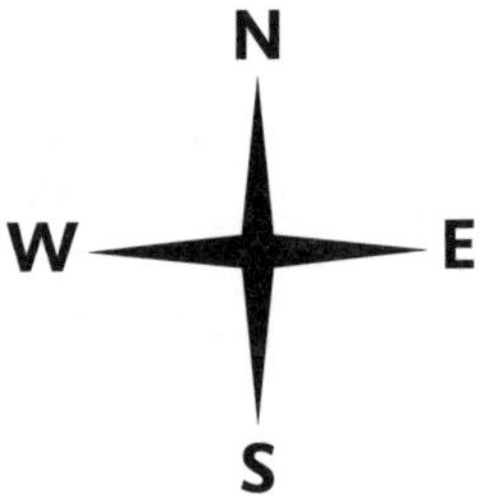

N
W —+— E
S

Now describe your route using compass directions.

★ Challenge

A walker leaves his campsite and walks north for a mile, west for three miles then south for four miles, east for two miles, north for two miles and east for a mile.

What direction does he need to travel to get back to the camp?
How far is it?

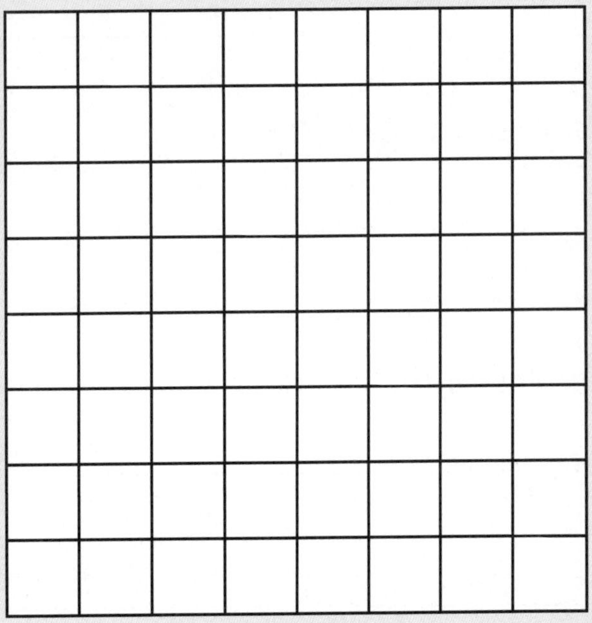

80

13.4 Grid references

1 a) Write down the grid reference for each shape.

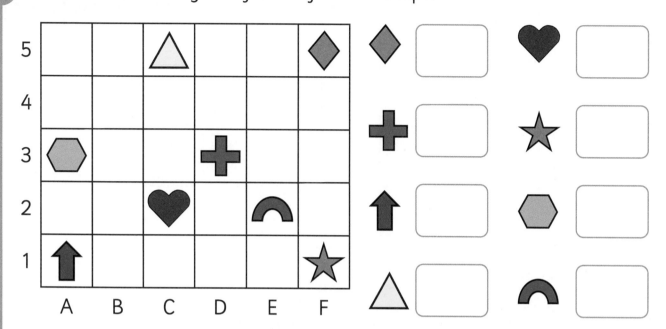

b) Draw these shapes in the correct square:

✗ in B4, ● in D2, ▮ in E4, ▼ in C3.

2 Plot these grid references by colouring the squares:

E4 – C2 – A2 – G3 – F4 – C1 – G1 – A3 – D2 – G2 – A4 – G4 – C3 – B2

5							
4							
3							
2							
1							

A B C D E F G H

What number have you made?

3

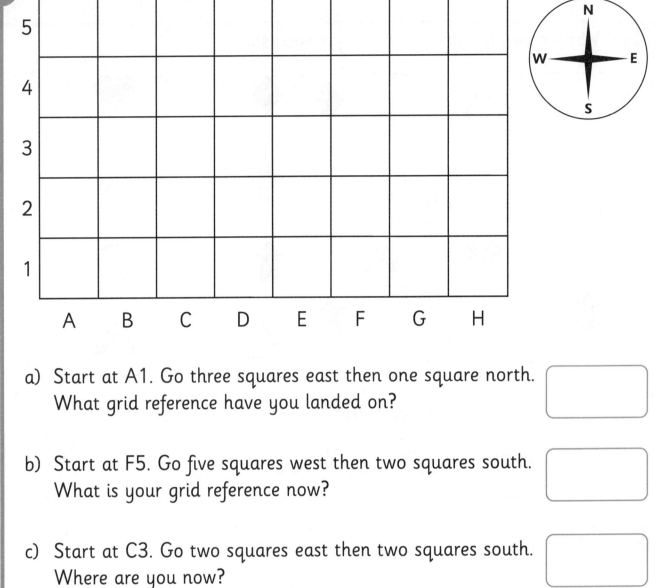

a) Start at A1. Go three squares east then one square north. What grid reference have you landed on?

b) Start at F5. Go five squares west then two squares south. What is your grid reference now?

c) Start at C3. Go two squares east then two squares south. Where are you now?

d) Start at G2. Go three squares north, five squares west and two squares south. What is the grid reference?

e) Start at C4. Go five squares east, two squares south, three squares west and three squares north. What is your new grid reference?

Now plot your answers in the grid above by colouring squares.

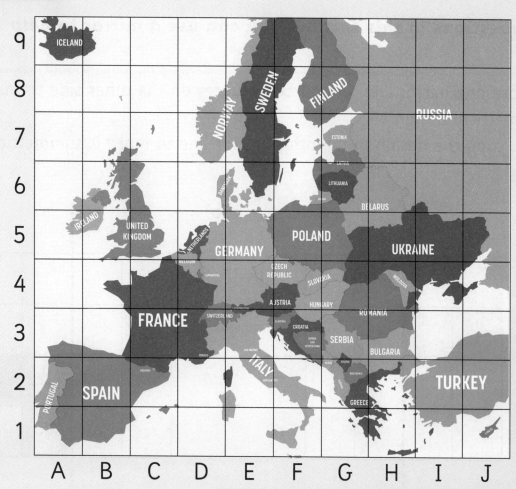

Which country or countries are within each grid reference?

a) B2 [   ]

b) J2 [   ]

c) C3 [   ]

Write directions to go from:

d) Cyprus (J1) to Lithuania (G6)

[   ]

e) Netherlands (D5) to Serbia (G3)

[   ]

For the questions in this section, you can use a mirror to help you.

1 Choose one mirror line. Colour the squares on the other side to make a symmetrical design.
Then copy the design in the other mirror line to make it symmetrical.

a)

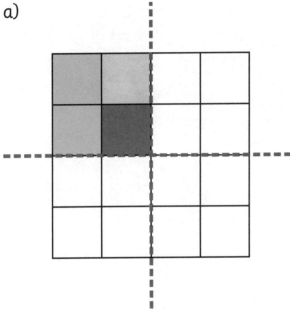

b)

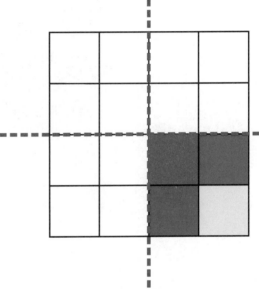

c)

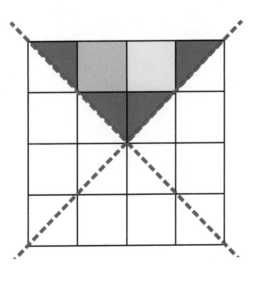

d)

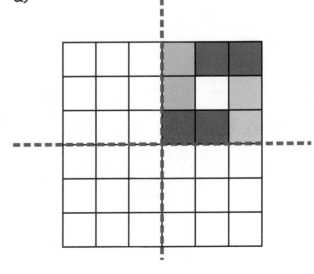

2 Use the grids to make your own designs with two lines of symmetry.

★ Challenge

Amman thinks this pattern has two lines of symmetry.

Isla thinks it only has one line of symmetry.

Finlay thinks it is not symmetrical.

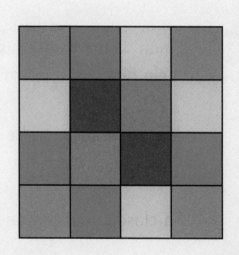

Who is correct? Explain why.

14.1 Collect, organise and display data

1 Tick the option which best describes the question.

a) Which computer games do you like playing? | open | closed |

b) Have you eaten one, two or three vegetables today? | open | closed |

c) Which is better, P.E. or maths? | open | closed |

d) How many books do you own? | open | closed |

e) Do you prefer water or milk? | open | closed |

f) How many rooms are in your house? | open | closed |

2 Amman wants to ask his classmates about their favourite computer games. To help him, write down:

a) an open question he could use.

b) a closed question he could use.

3 Isla wants to draw a chart to show what types of pets the children in her Brownie group have. Write down:

a) a closed question Isla could ask.

b) an open question Isla could ask.

c) Which question will be more useful to help Isla draw her chart? Explain why.

★ Challenge

Think of something you would like to ask the children in your class.

a) Write down one open and one closed question.

Decide which one you will ask.

b) Design a recording sheet to collect the data.

c) Use the sheet to gather and record the information, then use it to create a bar chart on squared paper.

1 a) Write each letter in the correct space to complete the Carroll diagram.

A   B   C   D   E   F   G

	No legs	Has legs
Fish		
Not a fish		

b) What do you notice?

2 a) Put these numbers into the correct places in the Venn diagram.

24   14   17   36   40   11   21   9   12   39

multiple of 2   multiple of 3

b) What do you notice about the numbers 17 and 11? Explain why this is the case.

a) Complete the Carroll diagram for children in your class.

	Likes maths	Does not like maths
Has brown eyes		
Does not have brown eyes		

b) Display the same information as a Venn diagram. Think carefully about how to label it.

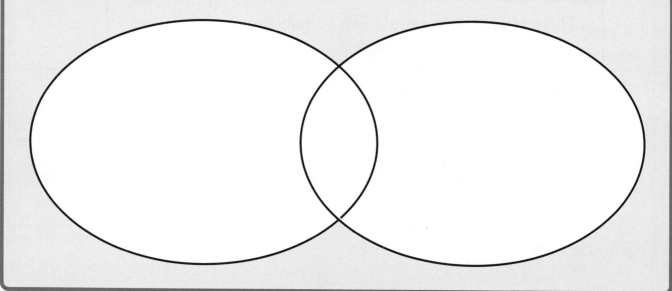

1 An ice cream shop wants to know which flavours of ice cream are most popular.

They collect data from their customers and make a bar chart.

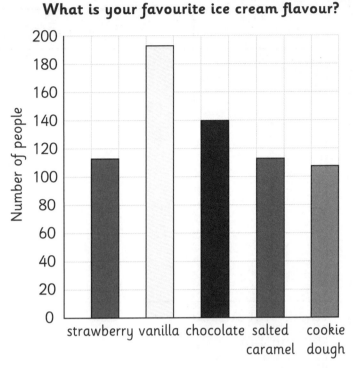

What is your favourite ice cream flavour?

a) Look at the bar chart and complete the table.

Statement	True	False
The least popular flavour is cookie dough.		
Chocolate is more popular than strawberry.		
The most popular flavour is salted caramel.		
Three times more people like vanilla than cookie dough.		
More people like salted caramel than strawberry.		

b) What else do you notice? Write a **true** statement of your own about the bar chart.

I notice that

2 Amman has drawn a line graph to track the money he has over an 8-week period.

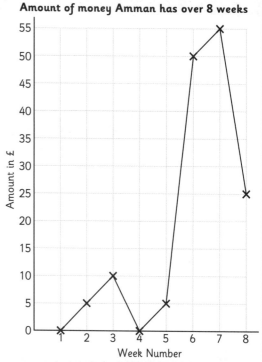

Amount of money Amman has over 8 weeks

Look at the line graph and tick whether each statement is true or false.

Statement	True	False
Amman has no money twice in eight weeks.		
Amman has twice as much money in week 8 than he does in week 3.		
The most amount of money Amman has is £50.		
Amman's money usually increases by £5 a week.		

★ **Challenge**

For each **TRUE** statement in **question 2,** make a conjecture and write it as a statement that begins "This could mean that ..."

1 Isla wants to know which clubs children at her school attend.
She conducts a survey. Here is a table showing the data she collected.

Club	Number of children P1–3	Number of children P4–7
Drama	8	24
Art	25	11
Sports	6	16
Dance	14	14
Choir	5	23

Complete the double bar graph to show her results.

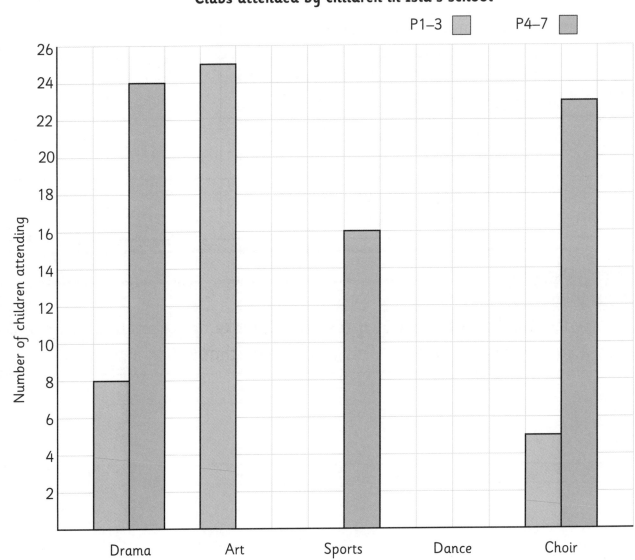

Clubs attended by children in Isla's school

P1–3   P4–7

Now answer these questions:

a) How many children attend Art Club altogether? ☐

b) Which club has the same number of children from P1–3 as P4–7?

☐

c) Which is the least popular club among P1–3?

☐

d) Which is the least popular club among P4–7?

☐

e) How many children attend either Dance Club or Sports Club? ☐

★ Challenge

You will need squared paper.

Carry out your own inquiry which will result in a double bar chart or a double line graph.

Remember you will be looking at data from two different sources.

Write some questions from your graph and ask a friend to answer them.

15.1 Using data to predict the outcome

1 Draw lines to connect each statement to how likely it is to happen on any school day.

There will be an indoor playtime.

A tiger will come to school.   **Will not happen**

Your teacher will speak.

There will be an assembly.   **Could happen**

Your teacher will be absent.

It will be a Sunday.   **Will happen**

You will eat lunch.

2 Look at the following events. Place the letters in the correct place on the probability scale, depending on their chances of happening this Saturday.

A   Your teacher will be eaten by a Tyrannosaurus Rex.

B   It will rain.

C   You will sleep in.

D   You will play a computer game.

E   Your head will fall off.

F   You will buy new shoes.

G   It will be Saturday.

H   You will eat breakfast.

impossible   unlikely   likely   certain

Compare with a partner. Were their answers the same?

3 Write down, or draw:

a) something that is impossible.

b) something that is certain.

c) something that is likely.

A bag contains ten marbles.

Eight of the marbles are blue and two are red.

Without looking, Finlay takes out one marble. The others predict the colour Finlay's marble is likely to be.

Isla thinks it is equally likely to be either red or blue, because both colours are in the bag.

Amman says it will certainly be blue because there are so many more blue marbles.

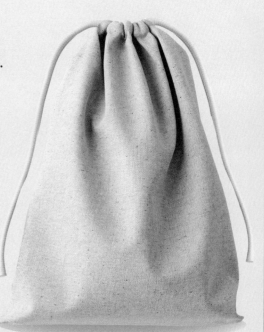

Nuria thinks it could be red, but is more likely to be blue.

Who do you agree with? Explain your thinking.